GRAPHIC HISTORY

HARRIET TUBMAN
and the
UNDERGROUND RAILROAD

by Michael Martin

illustrated by Dave Hoover & Bill Anderson

Consultant:
Lois Brown, PhD
Museum of Afro-American History
Boston, Massachusetts

Capstone
press

Mankato, Minnesota

Graphic Library is published by Capstone Press,
1710 Roe Crest Drive, North Mankato, Minnesota 56003.
www.capstonepub.com

Printed in the United States of America in Stevens Point, Wisconsin.

102012
007005R

Books published by Capstone Press are manufactured with paper containing at least 10 percent post-consumer waste.

Library of Congress Cataloging-in-Publication Data
Martin, Michael, 1948–
Harriet Tubman and the underground railroad / by Michael Martin; illustrated by Dave Hoover and Bill Anderson.
p. cm.—(Graphic library. Graphic history)
Includes bibliographical references and index.
Audience: Grades 4–6.
ISBN-13: 978-0-7368-3829-0 (hardcover) ISBN-10: 0-7368-3829-5 (hardcover)
ISBN-13: 978-0-7368-5245-6 (softcover pbk.) ISBN-10: 0-7368-5245-X (softcover pbk.)
1. Tubman, Harriet, 1820?–1913—Juvenile literature. 2. Slaves—United States—Biography—Juvenile literature. 3. African American women—Biography—Juvenile literature. 4. African Americans—Biography—Juvenile literature. 5. Underground railroad—Juvenile literature. I. Title. II. Series.
E444.T82M355 2005
973.7'115'092—dc22 2004015501

Summary: The story of Harriet Tubman and the Underground Railroad told in a graphic-novel format.

Editor's note: Direct quotations from primary sources are indicated by a yellow background.

Direct quotations appear on the following pages:
Pages 9, 11, 13, 15, 16, 23, from *Harriet Tubman: The Moses of Her People* by Sarah Bradford (Bedford, Mass.: Applewood Books, 1993).
Page 21, lyrics from "Steal Away to Jesus," an African American folk song, as quoted in *The Books of American Negro Spirituals* compiled by James Weldon Johnson and J. Rosamond Johnson (New York: Viking Press, 1940).
Page 27, from *Harriet Tubman* by Earl Conrad (Washington, D.C.: The Associated Publishers, 1943).

Art Director
Jason Knudson

Storyboard Artist
Keith Wilson

Colorist
Brent Schoonover

Editor
Donald Lemke

Acknowledgments
Capstone Press thanks Philip Charles Crawford, Library Director, Essex High School, Essex, Vermont, and columnist for *Knowledge Quest,* for his assistance in the preparation of this book.

Capstone Press thanks Dave Hoover and Bill Anderson of Cavalier Graphics.

TABLE OF CONTENTS

Chapter 1
Growing Up a Slave

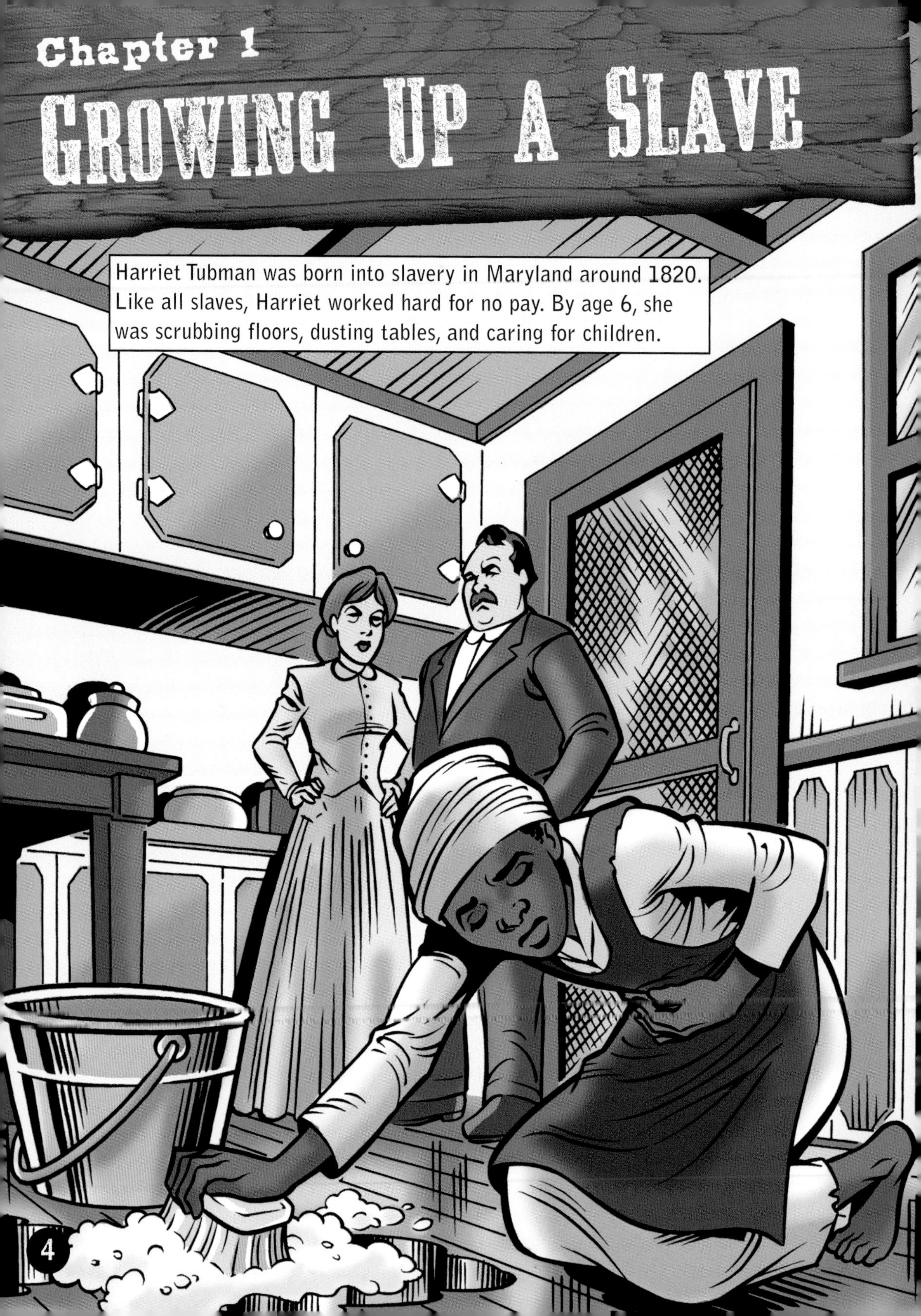
Harriet Tubman was born into slavery in Maryland around 1820. Like all slaves, Harriet worked hard for no pay. By age 6, she was scrubbing floors, dusting tables, and caring for children.

Slaves were the property of their owners. Harriet's owner, Edward Brodess, often rented her to other people. During these times, Harriet could not see her family and had little to eat.

I'm so hungry. No one will miss one lump of sugar.

Come back here, you lazy thief!

Harriet and other slaves wanted to escape these terrible conditions. But most runaway slaves were found and beaten.

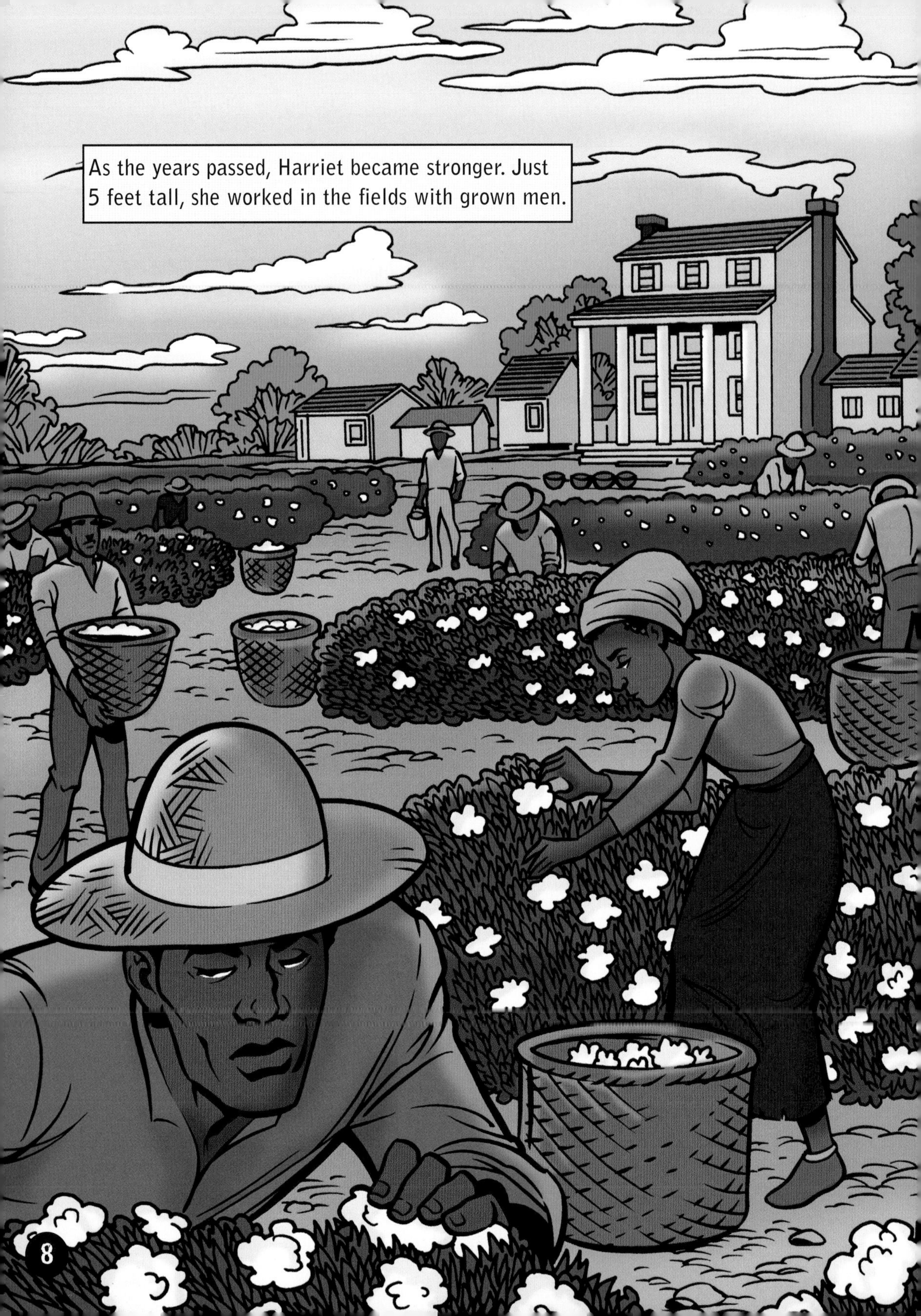
As the years passed, Harriet became stronger. Just 5 feet tall, she worked in the fields with grown men.

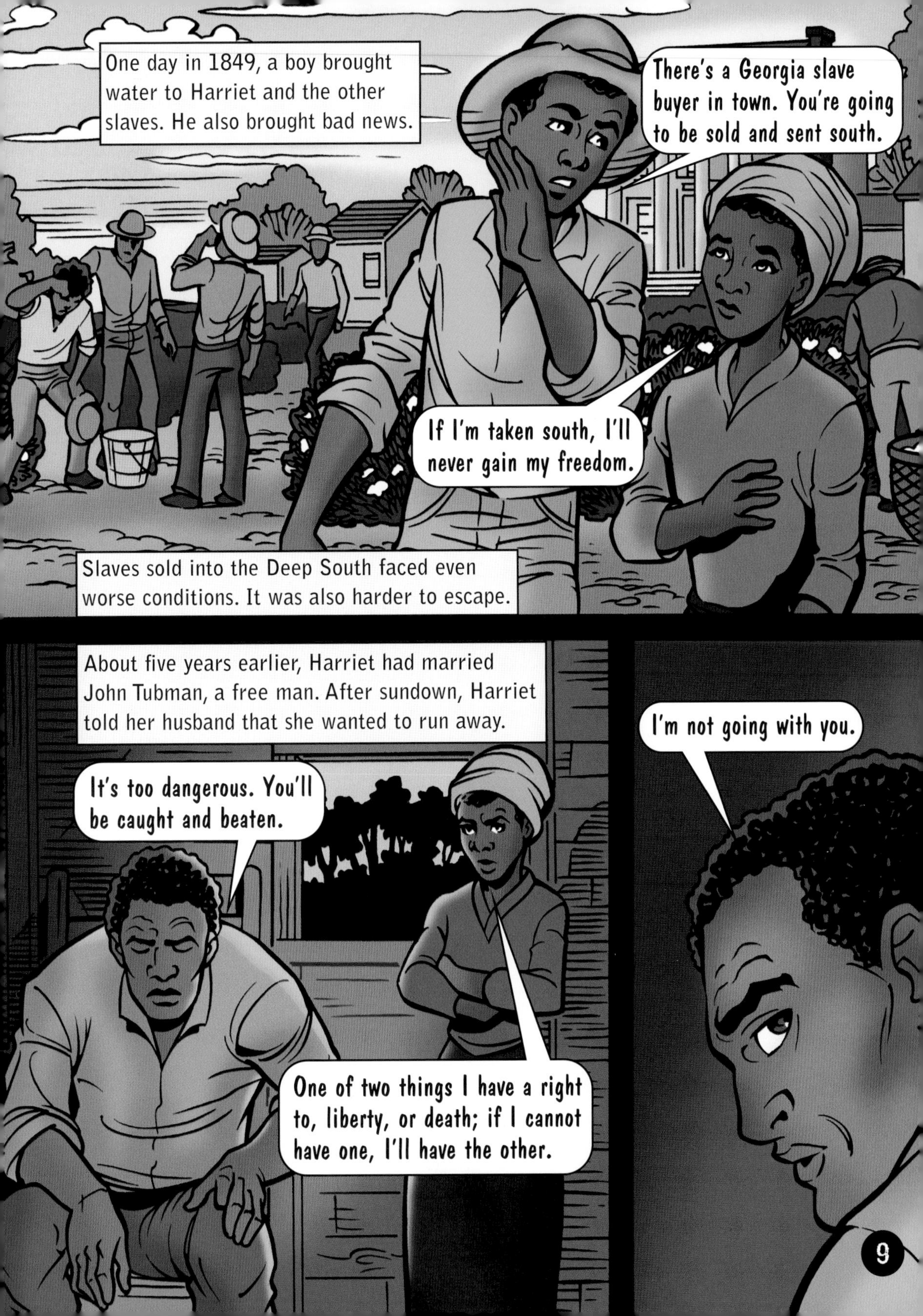
One day in 1849, a boy brought water to Harriet and the other slaves. He also brought bad news.
There's a Georgia slave buyer in town. You're going to be sold and sent south.
If I'm taken south, I'll never gain my freedom.
Slaves sold into the Deep South faced even worse conditions. It was also harder to escape.
About five years earlier, Harriet had married John Tubman, a free man. After sundown, Harriet told her husband that she wanted to run away.
It's too dangerous. You'll be caught and beaten.
One of two things I have a right to, liberty, or death; if I cannot have one, I'll have the other.
I'm not going with you.

Chapter 4
Conductor on the Railroad

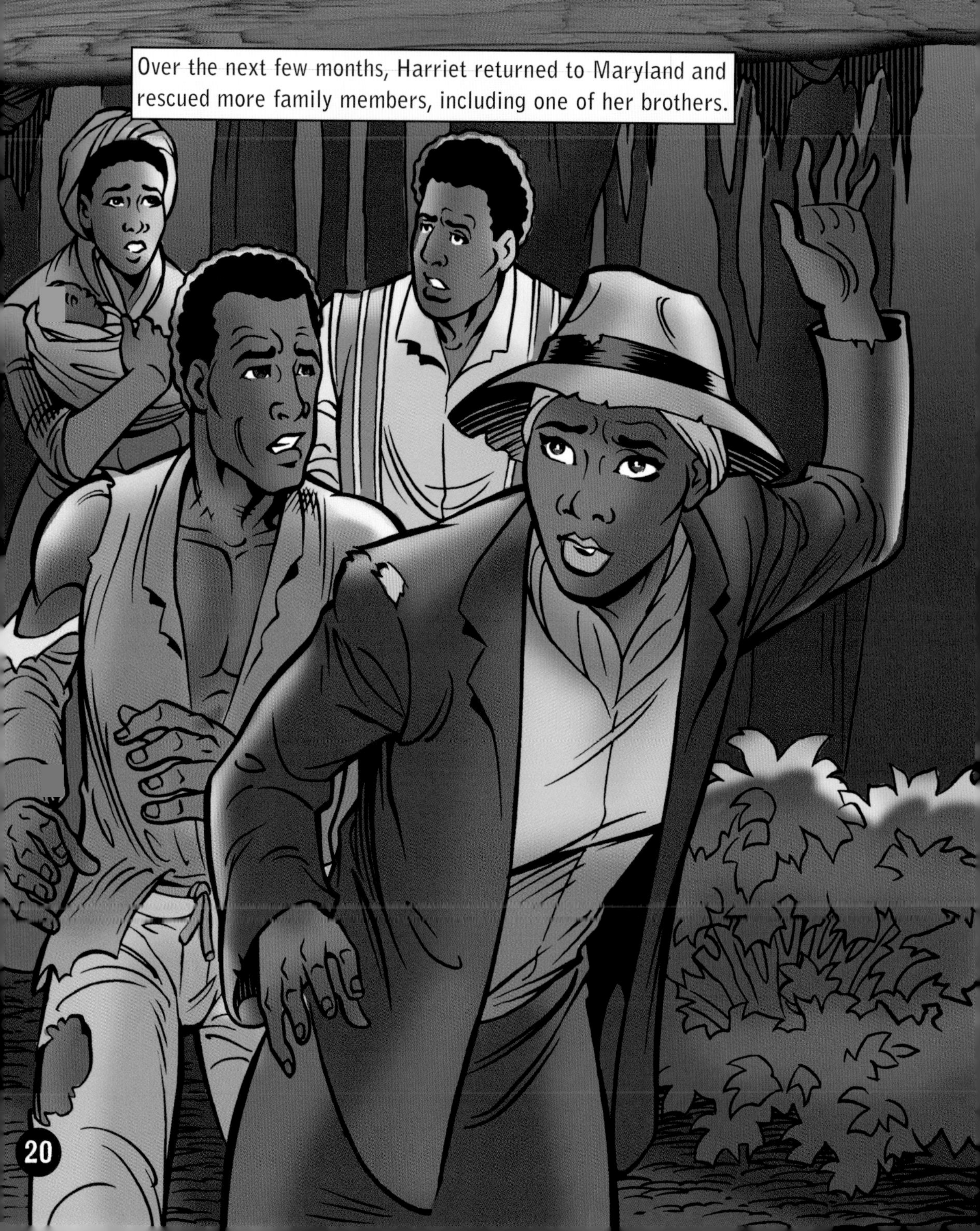
Over the next few months, Harriet returned to Maryland and rescued more family members, including one of her brothers.

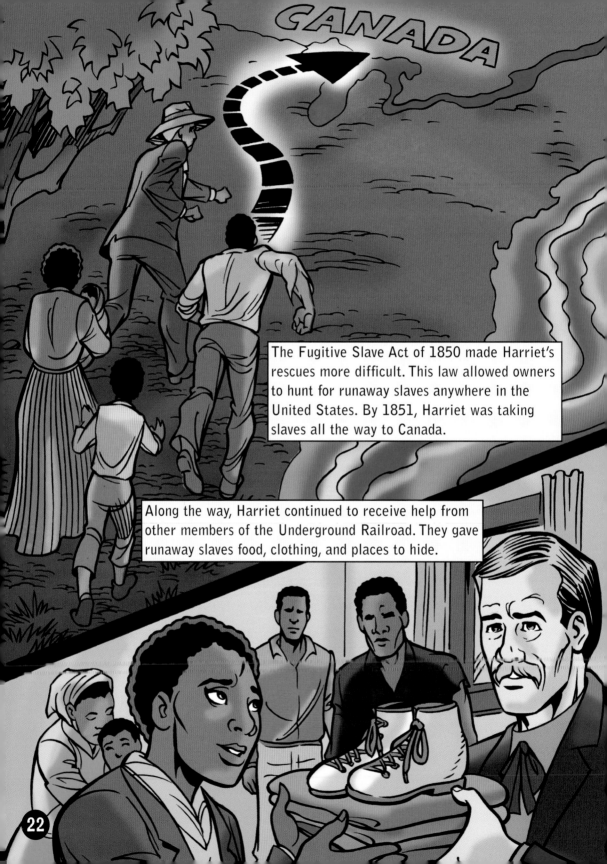

CANADA

The Fugitive Slave Act of 1850 made Harriet's rescues more difficult. This law allowed owners to hunt for runaway slaves anywhere in the United States. By 1851, Harriet was taking slaves all the way to Canada.

Along the way, Harriet continued to receive help from other members of the Underground Railroad. They gave runaway slaves food, clothing, and places to hide.

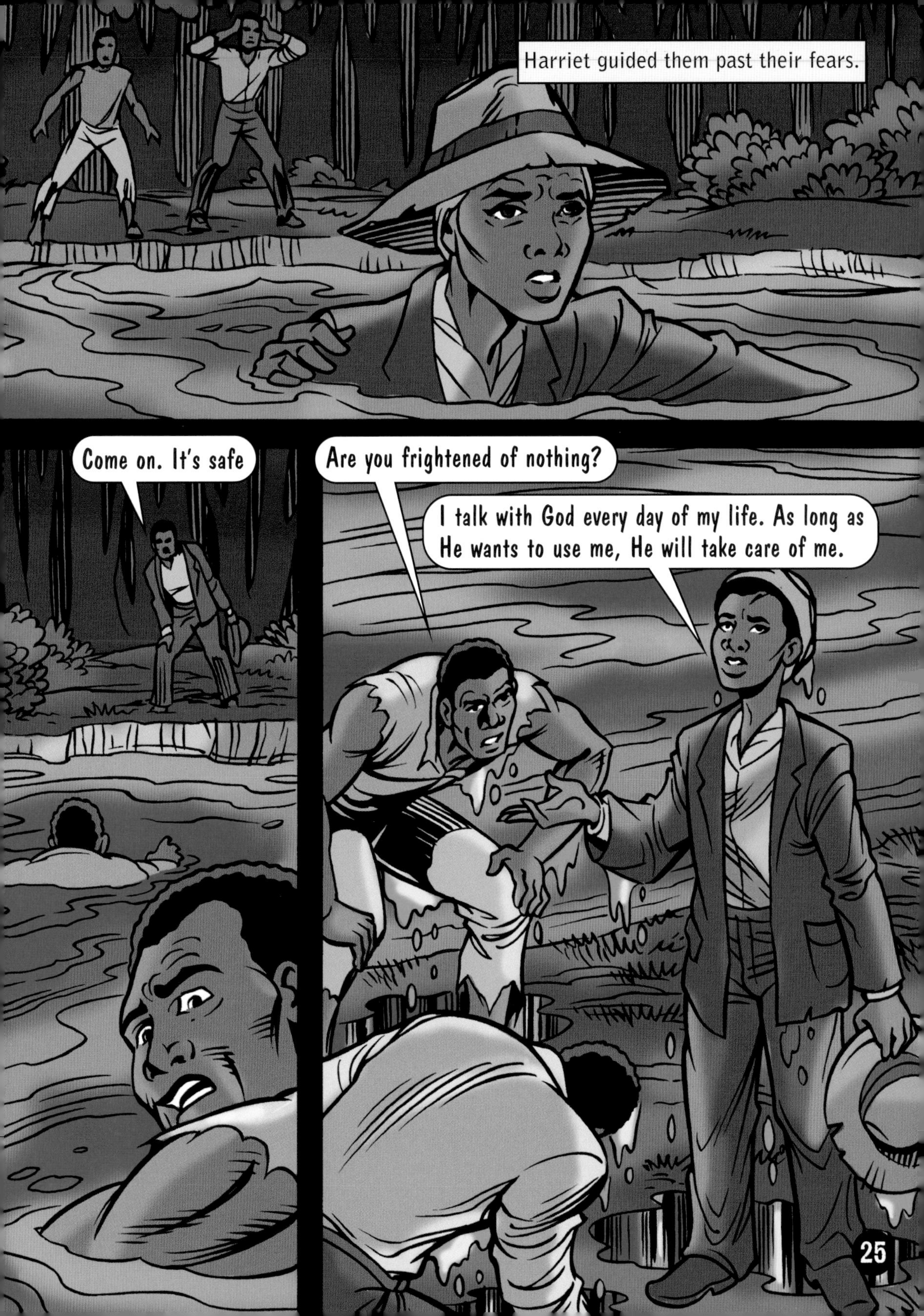
Harriet guided them past their fears.
Come on. It's safe
Are you frightened of nothing?
I talk with God every day of my life. As long as He wants to use me, He will take care of me.

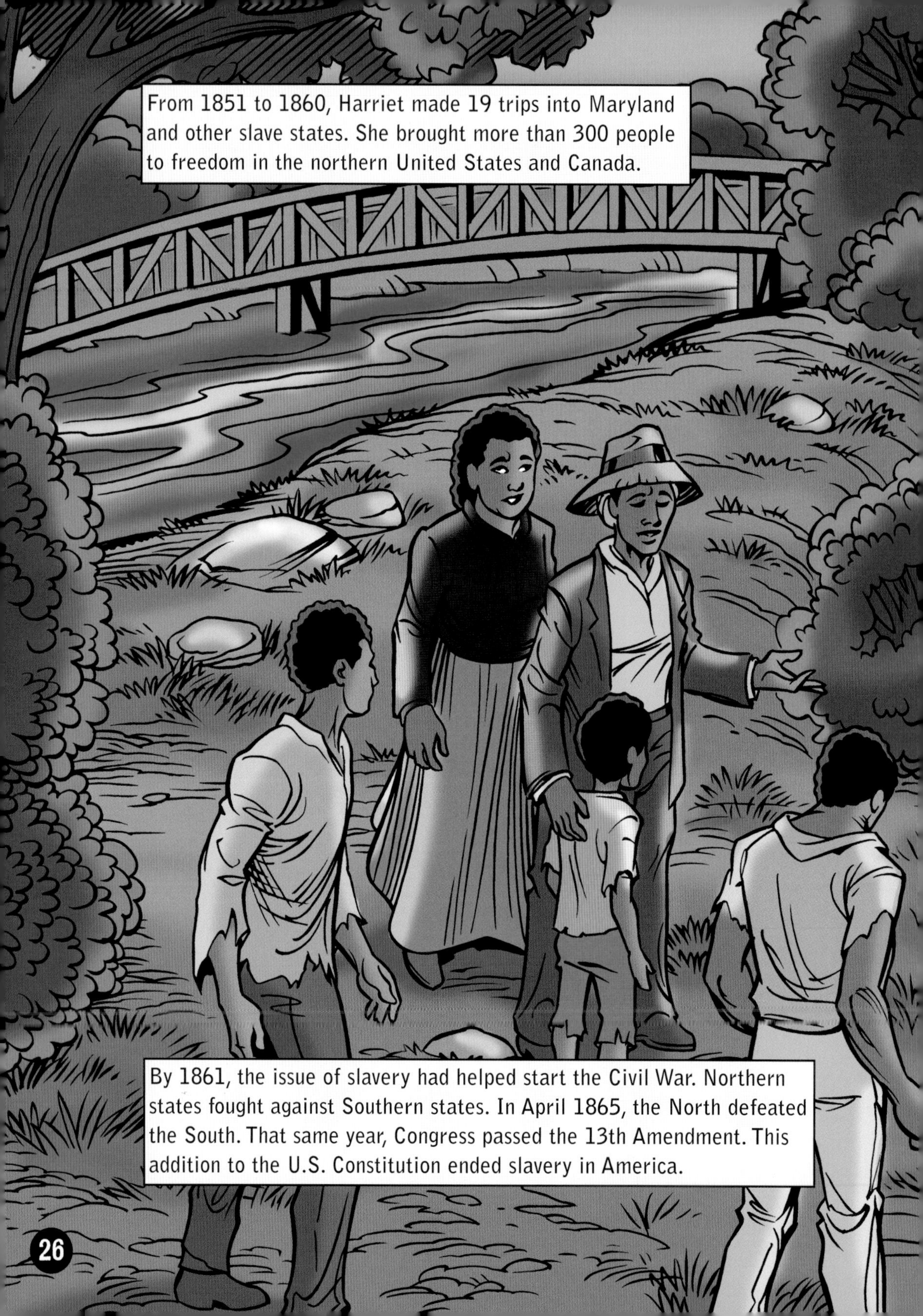
From 1851 to 1860, Harriet made 19 trips into Maryland and other slave states. She brought more than 300 people to freedom in the northern United States and Canada.
By 1861, the issue of slavery had helped start the Civil War. Northern states fought against Southern states. In April 1865, the North defeated the South. That same year, Congress passed the 13th Amendment. This addition to the U.S. Constitution ended slavery in America.

MORE ABOUT HARRIET TUBMAN

- At birth, Harriet Tubman was named Araminta Ross. Later, Harriet honored her family by taking her mother's first name.

- After her head injury, Harriet would faint or fall asleep several times a day. Harriet said she experienced visions of the future during many of these "spells." Some people believe that Harriet's visions helped her avoid being captured.

- Harriet used songs to send secret messages. Sometimes the songs warned runaway slaves of danger ahead. Harriet often sang "Wade in the Water" when slave catchers and their dogs were approaching. This song signaled runaway slaves to get off the trail and into a river or swamp. Walking through water would help throw the dogs off their scent.

- In 1851, Harriet returned to the South to find her husband, John Tubman. She wanted John to come with her to the North. Unfortunately, John had married another woman and did not want to leave.

- Harriet rescued many of her family members from slavery in the South. In 1857, she brought her parents north to freedom in St. Catharines, Ontario, Canada.

During one rescue, Harriet had a bad toothache. Instead of suffering with the pain, Harriet knocked out two of her teeth with a pistol.

During the Civil War, Harriet became a nurse for the Union army in the North. Later, she helped the army as a spy and a scout.

In 1863, Harriet led 150 Union soldiers on a raid in South Carolina. The troops freed 750 slaves and destroyed enemy supplies.

After the Civil War ended, Harriet headed for Auburn, New York. While living in Auburn, she worked with women's rights groups, raised money for schools, and helped in her church.

On June 23, 1908, Harriet opened the Harriet Tubman Home. This charity shelter helped older and ill African Americans in New York.

On March 10, 1913, Harriet died at her home in Auburn, New York. Since 1953, the Harriet Tubman Home has been a memorial to Tubman's life.

GLOSSARY

blackout (BLAK-out)—a loss of vision or memory for a short period of time

Congress (KONG-griss)—the government body of the United States that makes laws

Constitution (kon-stuh-TOO-shuhn)—the written system of laws in the United States that states the rights of the people and powers of the government

overseer (OH-vur-see-uhr)—a person in charge of watching and punishing slaves

slavery (SLAY-vur-ee)—the owning of other people; slaves are forced to work without pay.

station (STAY-shuhn)—a hiding place on the Underground Railroad

INTERNET SITES

FactHound offers a safe, fun way to find Internet sites related to this book. All of the sites on FactHound have been researched by our staff.

Here's how:

1. Visit *www.facthound.com*
2. Type in this special code **0736838295** for age-appropriate sites. Or enter a search word related to this book for a more general search.
3. Click on the **Fetch It** button.

FactHound will fetch the best sites for you!

READ MORE

Healy, Nick. *Harriet Tubman: Conductor to Freedom.* Fact Finders Biographies. Mankato, Minn.: Capstone Press, 2005.

Klingel, Cynthia Fitterer. *Harriet Tubman: Abolitionist and Underground Railroad Conductor.* Our People. Chanhassen, Minn.: Child's World, 2004.

Monroe, Judy. *The Underground Railroad: Bringing Slaves North to Freedom.* Let Freedom Ring. Mankato, Minn.: Bridgestone Books, 2003.

BIBLIOGRAPHY

Bradford, Sarah H. *Harriet Tubman: The Moses of Her People.* Bedford, Mass.: Applewood Books, 1993. A facsimile of *Scenes in the Life of Harriet Tubman.* Auburn, N.Y.: W.J. Moses, 1869.

Clinton, Catherine. *Harriet Tubman: The Road to Freedom.* Boston: Little, Brown, 2004.

Conrad, Earl. *Harriet Tubman.* Washington, D.C.: The Associated Publishers, 1943.

Humez, Jean McMahon. *Harriet Tubman: The Life and the Life Stories.* Madison, Wis.: University of Wisconsin Press, 2003.

Johnson, Weldon James, and J. Rosamond Johnson, comp. *The Books of American Negro Spirituals.* New York: Viking Press, 1940.

Larson, Kate Clifford. *Bound for the Promised Land: Harriet Tubman: Portrait of an American Hero.* New York: Random House, 2005.

INDEX